# STEVE JOBS

Also by Jessie Hartland

*Bon Appétit! The Delicious Life of Julia Child*

# STEVE JOBS

## insanely great

a graphic biography by jessie hartland

EMBER

Published in the United States by Ember, an imprint of Random House Children's Books,
a division of Penguin Random House LLC, New York.
Originally published in hardcover in the United States by Schwartz & Wade Books,
an imprint of Random House Children's Books, New York, in 2015.

Ember and the E colophon are registered trademarks of Penguin Random House LLC.

Visit us on the Web! randomhouseteens.com

Educators and librarians, for a variety of teaching tools, visit us at RHTeachersLibrarians.com

The Library of Congress has cataloged the hardcover edition of this work as follows:
Hartland, Jessie.
Steve Jobs : insanely great / Jessie Hartland. — First edition.
pages cm
Includes bibliographical references and index.
ISBN 978-0-307-98295-7 (alk. paper) — ISBN 978-0-307-98297-1 (ebook)
1. Jobs, Steve, 1955–2011—Juvenile literature. 2. Jobs, Steve, 1955–2011—Comic books, strips, etc. 3. Computer engineers—United States—
Biography—Juvenile literature. 4. Computer engineers—United States—Biography—Comic books, strips, etc. 5. Graphic novels. I. Title.
QA76.2.J63 H37 2015
338.761004092—dc23
[B]
2014005768

ISBN 978-0-307-98298-8 (trade pbk.)

Printed in the United States of America

10 9 8 7 6 5 4 3 2 1

First Ember Edition 2016

Random House Children's Books supports the First Amendment and celebrates the right to read.

This one's for
my son, Sam —
lover of apple pie
as well as those
other, nonedible
apple products.

# Contents

Here's to the crazy ones. The misfits. The rebels. The troublemakers. The square pegs in the round holes. The ones who see things differently. Because the people who are crazy enough to think they can change the world are the ones who do.

— S.J.

the journey
is the reward

—S. J.

**STEVE JOBS**

He was a tinkerer. He was willful and rebellious and did NOT like to follow rules.

He dropped out of college after just one semester and took a calligraphy class.

He started Apple Computer in his parents' garage and it became the world's most valuable company.

He was a techno-geek and an artist.

He brought us the COOL products everyone wants, and award-winning films like Toy Story, UP, and Finding Nemo.

How did such an iconoclast become the world's best business-man? This is the story.

*iPad*

Steve's Bench

# chapter

## 1

### The

### Young Sprout

### (1955 - 1965)

# Steve is born in San Francisco, California, in 1955.

His biological parents are unmarried college students.

They put Steve up for adoption.

Later, they marry and have a daughter, whom they raise; then they divorce.

# Steve is adopted by Clara and Paul Jobs.

Unable to have their own baby, they are ecstatic. Two years later, they adopt a girl, Patty.

Steve grows up in the Santa Clara Valley (now Silicon* Valley), south of San Francisco.

"a Likeler"

They live in a tract home inspired by the developer Joseph Eichler: simple, modern, suburban.

*a common element found in sand and glass, used in making high-tech devices

From an early age, Steve is mischievous. He is a rule-breaker, big-time. In elementary school he creates some posters.

Bring your PET to school day Tomorrow!

Ha Ha

P Q R S T U V W X Y Z

The next day is CRAZY!!

Paul Jobs is a machinist. He makes *prototypes* in the technology industry and his hobby is fixing up cars.

Steve and his dad like to tinker. Many weekends they visit the junkyard and pick up odds and ends for projects they make in their garage.

San Francisco

L A S E R

JUNK

where Hewlett-Packard was born

STANFORD University School of Engineering

101

NA Ames

Palo ALto

FAIRCHILD Semiconductor

RADAR

westing

Santa Clara* Valley in the early 1960s...

*now silicon valley

...is a busy, buzzing place with hundreds of technology companies employing thousands of people. The United States is in a cold war and a space race with the Soviet Union. The Russians live in a communist society, considered a threat to US capitalism.

Having launched Sputnik, the first satellite, in 1957, the Soviets are winning the space race. Scrambling to catch up, the US government is funding oodles of defense contractors who are experimenting with new space and weapons technology. These Silicon Valley businesses are part of what's called the military-industrial complex.

Steve's neighborhood is swarming with engineers who work at places like NASA, Westinghouse, and Lockheed Missile.

There is an exciting air of mystery and intrigue.

Companies that started out small inside home garages, like nearby Hewlett-Packard, are becoming giant. Tiny new companies are sprouting up in Steve's neighborhood.

One day they will be huge.

Steve and his dad make good use of their garage.

Steve even has his own workbench.

Steve learns at an early age that he is adopted.

Does that mean my REAL mom and dad didn't want me?

His parents reassure him:

Oh, no, honey.

You are special.

We love you very much.

But even with these re-assurances, the idea of abandonment will haunt Steve forever.

CHOSEN
SPECIAL
ABANDONED

In middle school, Steve's superior intelligence leads to general boredom and more mischief-making,

some dangerous. He is sent home from school many times.

Luckily, his 4th-grade math teacher notices

Algebra
GEOMETRY
CALCULUS
algebra 2
Analytic Geometry

his brilliance...

IMOGENE HILL

...and keeps STEVE challenged.

HIGH SCHOOL MATH
QUANTUM MECHANICS

Outgoing and always curious, Steve makes friends with some of the neighborhood engineers.

Steve, I'm glad you're here. Let me show you something.

COOL!

battery

carbon microphone

speaker

cool

cool

Hey, Dad! Mr. Lang can amplify using just a carbon mike, a battery, and a speaker!

No, son, that's not possible! You've got it wrong.

Gee whiz, my dad does not know everything.

See! I told you!

I'll be darned!

They don't come brighter than that, Paul.

see!

see!

SEE!

chapter

2

Growing Up
(1965 — 1971)

Things are pretty low-tech:

These vinyl discs, called records, hold just a few songs, and you play them on an electric...

The records are carried around in a case like this.

...record player.

Big records, called LPs, for "long-playing" — 33.3 revolutions per minute — have a small hole.

Tech

transistor radios

made in Japan

Small records, called 45s, for the spin speed — 45 RPM — have a big hole.

in

thingamajig

19

Games are all (candy Land) the board type.

These mini antennae are called rabbit ears.

Some TVs have a round screen.

Most TVs are just in B & W with no remote control.

I ♡ LOVE LUCY

(As with Wi-Fi now, the TV picture comes through the air.

18

All phones are the rotary-dial type with cords.

No cell phones!

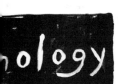

Cameras require film and developing.

If you have to write something official, you use a typewriter.

To correct mistakes, you use a special kind of eraser or paint.

CORRECT TYPE

No ONE has a computer in their home.

No Internet!

No Google.

If you want to learn about something, you have to...

...look in a book.

LIBRARY
LOS ALTOS

POPULAR ELECTRONICS

1962 1963 19
PM PM PM

POPULAR MECHANICS

physics projects
ELECTRICITY
machines
MUSIC
what's inside your HOUSE?
ART
aerodynamics
CHEMISTRY
Quantum mechanics

Physics

Sound

When Steve is 12, he decides to build a frequency counter,* which will help him with electronics projects.

* a device that measures the number of pulses per second in an electronic signal

But he's missing some critical parts. Steve is not shy. He looks up his neighbor, the cofounder of Hewlett-Packard, in the phone book.
May I please speak to Mr. Bill Hewlett?
OIL
Hewlett gives Steve the parts he needs and, when summer comes, offers him a summer job.

Steve works on an assembly line making frequency counters.

Over the next 3 summers, he has a newspaper route and works at a large electronics store.

HEWLETT-PACKARD

H-P

Star Trek

HALTEK

He saves his money and, when he is 15, buys his first car,

HALTEK

a Nash Metropolitan.

Steve grooves to the new music of the day.
BOB DYLAN
Grateful Dead
of the SUN
SURREALISTIC PILLOW
Jefferson AIRPLANE
Everybody must get...

He reads piles of books, both old and new.

He smokes pot and takes hallucinogenic drugs like L.S.D.

# The high school electronics class *is* outta sight!

Through a friend in the class, Steve meets another Steve— Stephen Wozniak, aka Woz.

Heathkits!

Fibonacci numbers!

BOB Dylan!

Hallicrafters!

Electronics pranks!

Frequency counters!

Boolean algebra!

The San Jose swap meet!

They have a lot in common.

By now, Steve is a high school senior.

Woz is 4 years older, and already in college nearby at UC Berkeley. He's a real techno-whiz, and is shy and sweet-natured.

**The** same year, Steve meets the girl who will become his first serious girlfriend.

Chrisann Brennan

They make an animated film together ...

... and with Woz get jobs entertaining children for $3 an hour

WESTGATE          SHOPPING          MALL

at a local shopping mall.

# Chapter 3

Steve and Woz
Start Their First
Business

(1971)

One day Steve and Woz read a magazine article called "Secrets of the Little Blue Box." A blue box is a homemade, cobbled-together device that replicates sounds the phone company uses to connect long-distance calls. It is illegal.

In 1971, making long-distance calls is really expensive.

A hacker nicknamed Captain Crunch outsmarts the phone company by imitating the crucial tones with a whistle he finds in a box of cereal.

Cap'n Crunch

Other phone phreaks

use exotic birds.

We can try and make our own version of the blue box.

According to this article, everything we need to know is explained in a tech journal you can get at the library.

Let's go!

These devices would not work with today's phone system.

The phone company has already asked all libraries to remove this journal from their shelves...

...or cut out the page with the tone codes.

But Steve and Woz know an obscure library that might have the publication intact.

STANFORD LINEAR ACCELERATOR

employee entrance

LIBRARY

They sneak in on a Sunday when the library is closed.

Do you think it will still be there?

Far out !!!

YES !!

Los Altos LIBRARY

They do some reading...

and some shopping...

sunnyvale electronics

and by Thanksgiving their blue box prototype is ready to test.

RADIO shack

Will it work?

34

Steve makes sure the blue boxes are "user-friendly" so that anyone can use them, not just techy types. They happily sell them here and there until something really bad happens...

chapter

4

COLLEGE

and

Enlightenment

(1972 - 1974)

Steve's parents want him to go to college, although Steve is not sure about the idea.

Steve, honey?

S.F. State

U.C. Berkeley

De Anza Comm. College

For financial reasons, they hope he'll choose an affordable public university.

He wants someplace artsy and only applies to one school — an expensive private one.

REED

In September 1972, Steve goes off to Reed College in Portland, Oregon.

REED

After one semester he drops out.

It's too expensive. And I want to study what I want to study, not all this other stuff.

Groovy.

I hear you, man.

Dan Kottke

38

Still, he hangs around Reed sitting in on some courses. He especially likes a calligraphy class.

serif

sans serif

baseline

x-height

ascender →

apple ←

descender

Fonts
A a @

A A

size: 28 pt
leading: 48 pt

nib →

INK

soda

return 5¢

To earn some money, he returns soda bottles and collects the deposits— 5¢ each.

1974

Steve leaves college and spends time on a commune on an apple orchard in Oregon.

He savors the art of pruning: cutting and trimming trees to make them grow stronger.

He becomes a vegetarian and eats so many carrots he turns orange! Because of this diet, he (wrongly!) believes he does not need to bathe much.

He gets hired as a technician for $5 an hour,

but because he never bathes, he is made the lone employee on the night shift.

Steve works on game design. Like all computer games in 1974, Atari games are simple: no instruction manual is needed.

ATARI

BE HERE NOW

1090

Steve really likes that.

circa **1970** coin-operated
computer games all in B&W only

PONG

First commercially
successful video
game. Like table
tennis on a screen.

SPACE RACE⊙

Two players
each control
a rocket ship,
avoiding
obstacles.

TANK

Players guide
their tanks
around a
maze, firing
at obstacles.

These games are played only in arcades, as people do not have home computers yet.

Ever since he was a teenager, Steve has looked at himself in the mirror every morning and asked,
If today were the last day of my life, would I want to do what I am about to do today?
And when the answer has been "no" for too many days in a row, he knows he has to change some-thing.
CRUST

48

After 7 months, Steve returns to California.
AIR INDIA
Steve— is that you?
can't be...
His parents do not recognize him.

chapter

5

Apple Is Born

(1975 — 1976)

Steve meditates in the mornings, audits physics classes at Stanford University in the afternoons, dreams of starting his own business, and goes back to work at Atari.

His boss offers much advice.

Pretend to be completely in control and people will assume you are.

Don't take **NO** for an answer.

Meanwhile, at Hewlett-Packard, Woz is frustrated designing calculators.

He has a new idea.

It's my prototype for something called a home computer.

Not interested.

It's not a serious computer.

It's just for hobbyists.

H-P may not like Woz's idea, but Steve does.

Insanely great, man! Let's start a business!

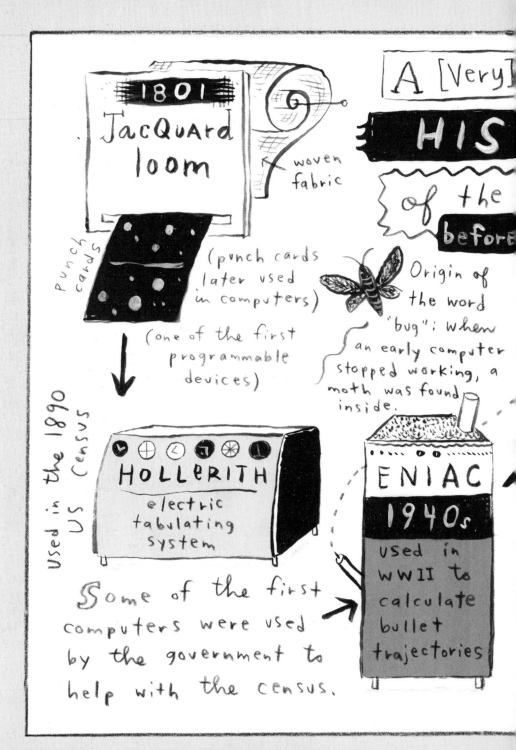

**1801**

**JacQuard loom**

woven fabric

Punch cards

(punch cards later used in computers)

(one of the first programmable devices)

A [Very]

HIS

of the

before

Origin of the word "bug": When an early computer stopped working, a moth was found inside.

Used in the 1890 US Census

**HOLLERITH**
electric tabulating system

**ENIAC**
**1940s**
used in WWII to calculate bullet trajectories

Some of the first computers were used by the government to help with the census.

# BRIEF

## TORY

### Computer
### 1975

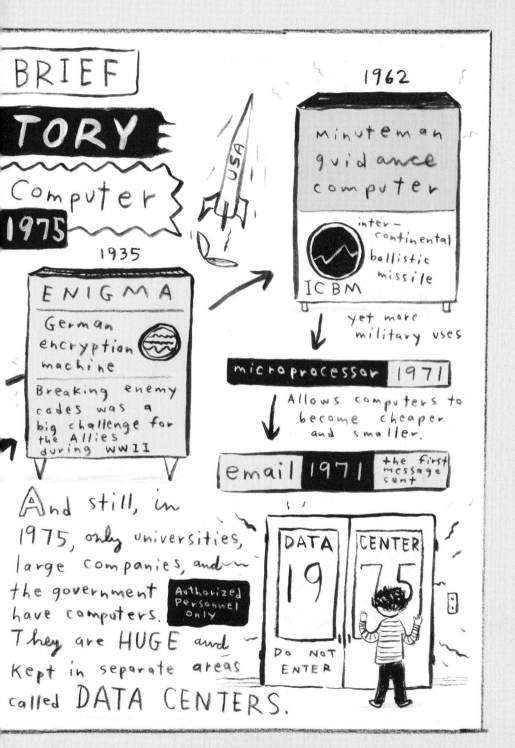

1935

**ENIGMA**

German encryption machine

Breaking enemy codes was a big challenge for the Allies during WWII

1962

**minuteman guidance computer**

inter-continental ballistic missile

**ICBM**

yet more military uses

**microprocessor** | **1971**

Allows computers to become cheaper and smaller.

**email** | **1971** | the first message sent

And still, in 1975, only universities, large companies, and the government have computers. **Authorized Personnel Only** They are HUGE and kept in separate areas called **DATA CENTERS.**

DATA CENTER 19 75

DO NOT ENTER

58

Almost no one has a computer at work or in their home.

In the early 1970s, powerful computers are HUGE, since memory takes up a lot of space. The ginormous computer shown here would hold only 8 megabytes* of memory.

In 2015, 64,000 megabytes fit in a cell phone.

2015

* more about bytes on pages 70-71

Slowly, companies are coming out with microcomputer kits.

But they tend to be for handy, techy scientist types...

require complicated assembly...

and don't really DO much.

They decide to raise money to buy parts to build a prototype.

Woz sells his Hewlett-Packard calculator for $500.

Steve sells his VW bus for $1,500.

Steve and Woz want their computer to be easy to use, nicely designed, AND inexpensive—

like the simple, modern home Steve grew up in.

65

Another friend does the bookkeeping.

Dan packs the assembled computers into boxes...

...after they've been tested by Dad.

Steve delivers the finished product.

Here it is —
**APPLE 1 computer**

The processor is the brain of the computer.

Memory is where data and instructions are stored.

A program is a sequence of instructions a computer can interpret and execute.

Pixel is short for "picture element." Pixels are the dots that make up each image.

A
P
P
L
E

There is heavy use of the arrow keys to get where you want to be on the screen — no one has invented the mouse yet.

So tedious!

Graphics are crude in 1976, because unlike today, the pixels are HUGE.

H
O
U
S
E

D
O
G

Images are mostly in black-and-white. Very few colors, if any.

One byte is one character — like a 1 or a Z or a %.

An operating system (OS) is the master program that runs the whole computer.

Booting up means loading software from the disc/tape into RAM memory.

a Koa wood case made by a local cabinet maker

**\* RAM \***
(random-access memory) is where programs actually "run."

**\* ROM \***
(read-only memory) are the programming routines that are "burned" into permanent memory.

one kilobyte (KB) is 1,024 characters—roughly one page of text.

one megabyte (MB) is 1,048,576 characters—roughly a whole book.

one gigabyte (GB) is 1,073,741,824 characters. Roughly 1,000 books—a whole shelf.

one terabyte (TB) is 1,099,511,627,776 characters. Roughly 1,000,000 books—a whole library.

Chapter

6

Moving Up

(1977)

The Apples are selling, but only to a limited market of hobbyists and other techy types. ①

Steve and Woz understand that for their company to grow, they need to make some changes. So...

TECH-O   H-P   TECH

...they hire more people. Engineers, programmers.

There are now 12 employees. ③

They rent office space nearby,

SONY   APPLE computer   WEIG LOSS   COMING SOON   APPLE

in Cupertino. ④

Because they need more money, they find an investor.

MIKE MARKKULA

Apple is now valued at #5,309. ⑤

Markkula will give them cash in exchange for part ownership of Apple.

⑥

74

Steve is 21 years old; Woz is 26. Markkula, 34, has already retired from the tech industry — a millionaire. He is good at marketing and sales and will help them get their business going.

Steve really likes his attitude.

You know, you should never start a company with the goal of getting rich. Your goal should be making something you believe in and building a company that will last.

For the next Apple, Steve wants to break out of the hobbyist market and design a computer that will appeal to a wider audience. It should fit in an attractive case and have a built-in keyboard. This has never been done before.

Steve goes to the mall to study the design of small kitchen appliances.

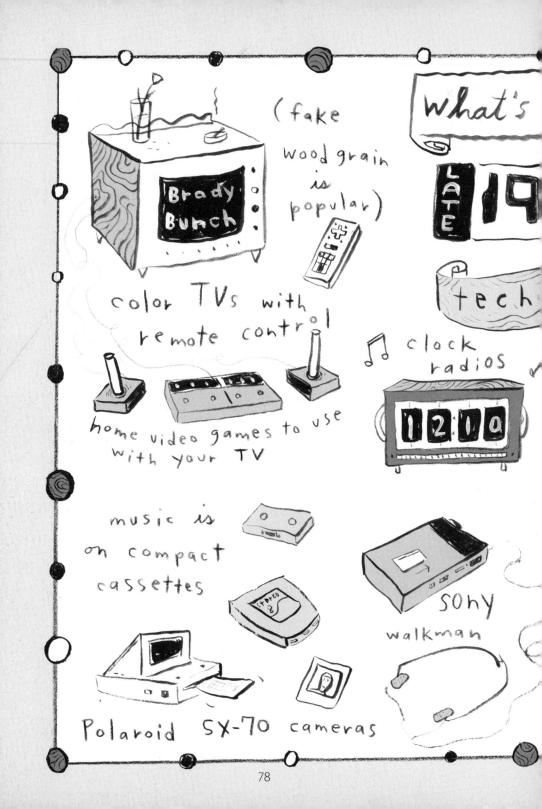

(fake wood grain is popular)

Brady Bunch

what's

LATE 19

tech

color TVs with remote control

clock radios

🎵

1210

home video games to use with your TV

music is on compact cassettes

STEREO 8

sony walkman

Polaroid SX-70 cameras

Meanwhile, using all his wizardry, Woz is designing the INSIDE of the computer, figuring out how to make it work better—and faster.

He has finally quit his job at Hewlett-Packard.

Boys, you need a marketing plan, a logo, etc.

You can't keep peddling these things door-to-door, you know.

Steve and Woz hire a publicity firm to help them promote their company.

blue

Regis McKenna

A designer named Rob Janoff designs a logo.

It has rainbow stripes.

green

Pink Steve likes this quote, thought to come from artist Leonardo da Vinci:

"Simplicity is the ultimate sophistication"

yellow

84

Woz has become a lot less involved in Apple.

After recovering from a flying accident, he decides to go back to college.

Steve and Woz have launched the entire personal computer industry, thanks to ingenuity, hard work, and being in the right place at the right time. By the end of 1978, Apple's sales are over $7.9 million.

Over the next 16 years, close to 6 million Apple IIs will be sold!

# Chapter

# 7

## Moving
## On

## (1978 – 1981)

In May 1978, Steve has a baby girl with his old girlfriend Chrisann. But he's irritated with the responsibility and

The baby's name is Lisa.

does not want to be involved.

He wants only to focus on his new business

and think about the next computer.

1979

The Apple II is not going to be a hit forever.

How to improve it?

All across the US, and especially in Silicon Valley, many companies — big and small — employ scientists, engineers, and designers in research labs.

IBM

XEROX PARC

DEC

BELL LABS N.J.

NASA AMES

They are all busy developing ideas for the office of the future. Xerox PARC* is in the forefront — even though they're not known for making computers.

*Palo Alto Research Center

Steve hears about some of these ideas.

We've gotta get over to PARC.

Xerox PARC WOW amazing NEW Scientific American

Bill Atkinson, Apple engineer

At about the same time, Xerox's venture capital division in Connecticut gives Apple a call. Like many, they want to invest in the hot new computer company.

Steve licks his chops.

OK—So here's the deal: I'll let you invest a million dollars in Apple if you show us what's going on at Xerox PARC. You gotta share everything with us.

No problem.

The Connecticut office has no idea how valuable Xerox PARC's research is.

Xerox buys 100,000 shares at about #10 each. A year later, Xerox's shares of Apple will be worth #17.6 million, almost $50 million in today's dollars.

Still, Apple gets the better part of the deal.

Steve and his crew drive 15 minutes north from Cupertino to Palo Alto.

As promised, the scientists show him what they've been working on.

These are all brand-new ideas to make the computers of the future simpler and easier to use. They are groundbreaking!

regions

bitmapping

MOUSE

wysiwyg

overlapping windows

xerox ALTO

What
You
See
Is
What
You
Get

I can't believe Xerox isn't pushing their own Xerox Star computer, with all these cool features, into the consumer market. They're sitting on a gold mine!
The corporate office is out of touch! They're just thinking about copiers.
Cupertino
Stevens Creek Boulevard
101
We can do a lot with this!
And they do. These new ideas will get used in Apple's next computer.

1980 By September, 130,000 Apple IIs have been sold.

APPLE

There are now more than 1,000 employees, and the company occupies 15 buildings.

With the new technology and ideas from Xerox PARC, and a new computer in the works, it's time to GO PUBLIC.

for SALE

$

Apple is a highly successful young company with thousands of loyal users, and people clamor to buy shares of stock.

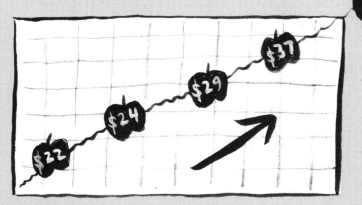

Apple's value goes up quickly. By the end of December, it is valued at $1.79 BILLION.

However, he continues to live simply. The brash young entrepreneur surrounds himself with just a few well-designed things.

CHAPTER

8

RISE and FALL

(1982 - 1986)

Long a follower of Zen Buddhism and a great admirer of the Japanese design aesthetic, Steve travels to Japan...

and appreciates the serenity and sublime order of the temples and gardens of Kyoto...

and the busyness and zaniness of Tokyo.

KABUKI　NIKON　NOH　東京　NHK　UC　SONY
SHINJUKU　SEIBU　GINZA　TOKYU HANDS
SUSHI　PACHINKO　Ueno　SHIBUYA　YAKITORI

He goes to a pristine Sony factory and sees
the workers all in uniform...

... and finally to see designer Issey Miyake,

Konichiwa!

who designs for Steve a...

Steve's main focus now is Apple's next computer.
He's concerned with the inner workings:
Larry, it's taking too long to boot up.
Steve, it's because—
If it could save a person's life, would you find a way to shave ten seconds off the boot time?
well, yeah, but—
If there are 5 million people using our computer, and it takes 10 seconds extra to turn it on, that adds up to 300 million or so hours — or 100 lifetimes — wasted!

Steve is still concerned with the OUTSIDE of the computer. He's becoming even more involved with the design.

* see page 118

Work continues, but these are harder times for Apple. Other companies, like IBM, have entered the personal computer industry.

# PC
## by
## IBM

P

V

AP

CIR
19

* has the big, established IBM name

* has decent word processing

* the favored model of large businesses, as it can connect and communicate with IBM minis and HUGE mainframe computers

software a set of programs that give instructions to a computer, telling it what to do and how to do it

APPLE II

* has VisiCalc, a terrific program for visualizing spreadsheets

* offers pioneering programs for writing and making music

* has games, graphics, and educational software

* the favored model of schools and universities

hardware) the physical pieces of a computer

While Steve knows himself to be quirky, tactless, confrontational, and insensitive, he knows Sculley is polite, polished, and easygoing. These qualities could help Apple grow and deal with competition from other computer companies.

I'm pretty happy working for Pepsi! And I don't know anything about computers.

Sculley finds Steve brilliant and fascinating. He's flattered that Steve wants him at Apple and decides to change jobs.

 Sculley comes on board, but right away there are disagreements.

Being the boss of an established soda company is mostly about putting out the same product year after year. Running a high-tech company is about improving, innovating, and trying to come up with the next big thing.

After years of delays, the new computer is about to be launched. What to call it?
Pippin? Red delicious? WINESAP? Macoun? Idared? Granny Smith?
APPLES
APPLE varieties

The year is 1984. An ad is sketched out by the director of <u>Blade Runner</u>, one of the most talked-about movies of that time.

This is INSANELY GREAT!

APPLE ... Ridley Scott ... 1984

This is called a storyboard.

I'm all for advertising during the Super Bowl, but this ad idea is nuts. And for ###? And it would only air ONCE?

Typical TV ads for computers depict boring real-life scenarios.

Household bills and accounting!

Or are whimsical spots using a clown.

IBM

Steve wants his ad to show the world how Apple products are tools for creativity, COOL and slightly rebellious!

The inspiration for the new Apple commercial is George Orwell's novel about a...

...totalitarian future society of government surveillance, constant war, and

mind control headed by the tyrannical leader Big Brother.

Steve gets his way...

... and when the ad is aired, it's called

A sensation!

The greatest commercial ever made!

On January 24, Apple Computer will introduce Macintosh. And you'll see why 1984 won't be like 1984.

Here it is!
the first MACINTOSH!
It's revolutionary!
hello
Hackers cannot break open the case and mess around!
Even more user-friendly and affordable!
* This is a beveled edge.
* This is a chamfer.
note the clean, soft lines
And in a fond nod to calligraphy at Reed, and for the first time: oodles of delightful fonts!
the commercia
to have

Macs sell well right from the start, but Apple is facing increased competition from other companies. Most aggressive is Microsoft, a software-only business led by the young Bill Gates.

microsoft

apple

NeRdY

StYliSH

born in 1955

born in 1955

Company produces only software

college dropout (Harvard)

college dropout (Reed)

Company makes hardware AND software

★ BiLL GATES ★

★ STEVE JoBS ★

Apple has approximately 6,500 employees now, roughly 700 in the Mac division.

Steve considers this new role.

But he decides he can't live with a smaller role in the company HE founded.

He becomes so nasty and unreasonable, so difficult to work with, that in the end, the board members and other employees choose Sculley as boss.

125

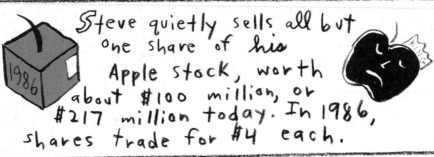

Steve quietly sells all but one share of his Apple stock, worth about #100 million, or #217 million today. In 1986, shares trade for #4 each.

At 30 years old, he is a very rich man — but rather miserable, too.

He travels to Europe, thinking about what to do NEXT...

How about starting a new company called NeXT?

The new computer will be a CUBE.

The logo is a CUBE, too...

I'm Paul Rand! ...designed by a famous designer. Steve pays #100,000.

It will be much faster than a PC and be able to do more things.

The company has 8 employees.

The target market is university research labs.

Sony Walkman ever more popular as it now plays CDs.

CDs

(over 250 million of these are sold)

wha

NE

19

Cable T.V 500 channels!

FAX machines

Telephone answering machines have hit the mainstream

Watching movies at home on a VCR (videocassette recorder)

VCR

Same VHS tape works in a camcorder

camcorder

Nintendo home games

128

NeXT struggles. Steve's perfectionism delays and delays the on-sale date of the computer.

chapter

9

the

Family

MAN

(Mid-1980s to Early 1990s)

Joanne has never told Mona about Steve and calls her at work.

1989 As the CEO of NeXT Computer,

STANFORD Business SCHOOL

Steve is asked to give a talk.

While he is waiting to go onstage, he meets a young Stanford business student.

She jokes,

I won a raffle and YOU get to take me out to dinner after your talk.

Oh, yeah?

But afterward, Steve has a business meeting to rush to.

bye

bye

As he is about to leave, he thinks,

If this were my last night on earth, would I want to spend it at a meeting or with this woman?

Ooo

134

135

She's a down-to-earth vegetarian, and very grounded, too; a good balance for Steve's eccentricities.

They marry in 1991, and later that year their son, Reed, is born.

Steve's daughter, Lisa, now 13, has become a part of the family, too.

They all live fairly simply in an old house in Palo Alto.

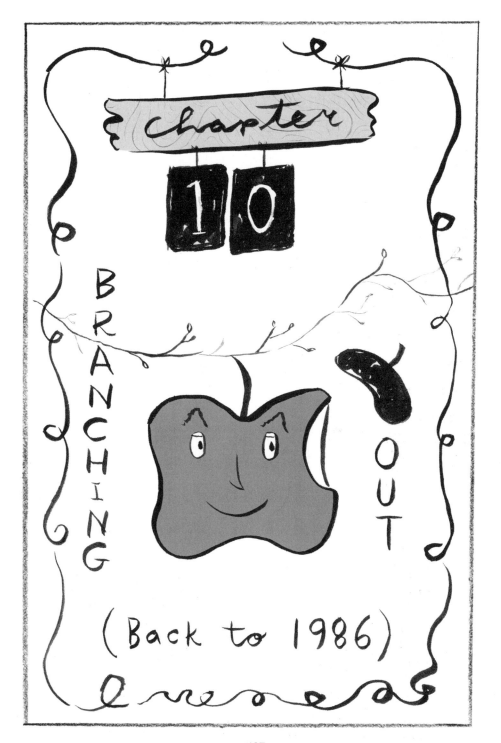

chapter

# 10

BRANCHING OUT

(Back to 1986)

While still running NeXT, which is tanking, Steve buys Pixar for #5 million (#10.7 million today) and immediately invests another #5 million to keep it going.

Art and technology together — just what I love!

Zillions more colors and pixels than most computers.

It's a small, pioneering computer graphics company that makes fancy computers and the software to go with them.

RenderMan

Animation on a computer!

#30,000

I think there's a market! Everyone will want one!

Images can be rendered in 3-D.

But the computers are VERY expensive and don't sell.

Steve keeps pouring his own money into the company to keep it afloat.

The short film, called *Luxo Jr.*, about a lamp, wins some awards.

SIGGRAPH* BEST Film 1986

HAWAII

*an annual computer graphics conference

Pixar gets new business creating animation for TV commercials. But not enough. The company is going broke.

The little 5-minute film — about toys that come to life — wins the Oscar for Best Animated Short Film, the first computer-animated film to do so.

OSCAR
ANIMATED
SHORT Film
1988

Disney is very excited about this new kind of animation and tries to woo former employee Lasseter back.

Sorry, I'm loyal to Pixar now.

145

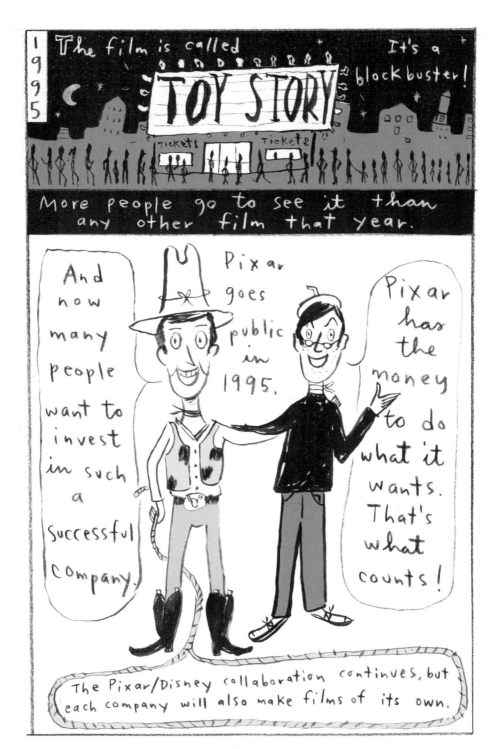

146

Steve's Pixar stock is now worth an astonishing #1.2 BILLION.

But Steve continues to live simply.

There's no yacht in my future.* I've never done this for the money!

* Ha! See pages 206 - 207

When Pixar expands, Steve designs their new building with a huge central atrium for workers to meet and mingle.

atrium

**2006** The contract between Pixar and Disney is coming to an end.

While Disney/Pixar have released megahits, Disney on its own has made multiple animation megaflops.

PIXAR FINDING | PIXAR NEMO | DISNEY BROTHER | DISNEY BEAR

CROWDS | Tickets | Tickets

The new Disney CEO approaches Steve and wants to buy Pixar.

Robert Iger

Steve puts together a clever deal and Disney buys Pixar for $7.4 billion.

Pixar gets stronger.

Disney gets better.

Wow, Dad!

Awesome!

Insanely great!

PIXAR RATATOUILLE DISNEY 2007

Disney/Pixar goes on to win more than 25 Academy Awards. It has become the most successful animation studio in the world.

chapter

11

The Return
to Apple
(1997 - 2001)

1997 Steve is still running a booming Pixar and a tanking NeXT.

Meanwhile, back at Apple...

Without Steve Jobs, the company is failing.* Sculley is long gone, as are several other CEOs. IBM's computers and Microsoft's Windows software now dominate the market.

CEO WANTED Apply within

*In fiscal year 1997, Apple loses $1.04 billion.

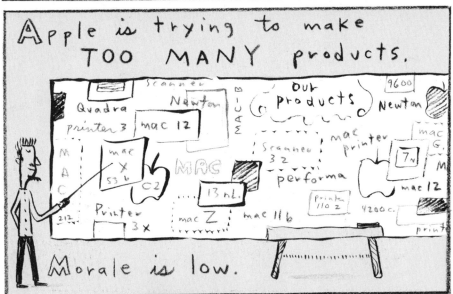

Apple is trying to make TOO MANY products.

Our products

Morale is low.

And because Apple likes the innovative way

Insanely great!

the NeXT computers work, it buys NeXT.

Everyone assumes Steve will play a minor role,

but . . .

pop

Of course, everyone at Apple remembers how difficult Steve can be, but they also remember his vision and his creativity.

Badly managed Apple is now close to bankruptcy, and the board of directors and employees are pretty desperate. Initially a part-time advisor, Steve is soon given more and more power.

Steve remembers how he went overboard at Apple the first time, and at NeXT, and now strives to make more rational decisions.

Out go the Apple printers and scanners, the redundant Quadra and Performa Macs, and the Newton, an early tablet.

What's with all these Macs?

Which one should I tell my friends to buy?

158

More drawings are made on paper...

...designs are made on computer,

and 3-D models are formed by an amazing machine!

3-D model-o-MATIC!

And finally, extensive research is done

Jelly Bean Factory

Jelly Belly

on color translucency.

Here it is →

DESIGN STUDIO

The people who are crazy enough to think they can change the world are the ones who do.

THINK Different

Think Different

groundbreaking ad campaign featuring celebrities and other influential people

a candy-colored, translucent, mouth-watering, jelly bean-influenced, cheeky, scrumptious, good-enough-to-eat, brand-new iMac!

The price is $1,299.

New iMac

What's late

boxy monitor

email really hits mainstream

DVDs

Klutzy CD tray

Google is founded.

www is growing rapidly.

digital cameras

NEW!
1990s

SONY

SONY
PlayStation

FILM
netflix
DVDs by Mail

eBay
online
auction

Mobile phones are smaller and more affordable but complicated to use.

a complicated mess of portable music players

SONY MD

RIO 300

mini discs

MP3 is a compressed digital format.

As work continues, Steve has an idea to open stores that sell only Apple products.

He wants to control the Apple customer's shopping experience.

Steve, maybe we should have a focus group?

Test out the market and see if people might actually shop in an Apple store or buy one of these?

Did Alexander Graham Bell do any market research before he invented the TELEPHONE?

And Henry Ford liked to say, "If I'd asked them what they wanted, they would have told me, 'A faster horse!'"

APPLE STORE

Steve secretly builds a store prototype inside a warehouse and makes regular visits to fine-tune the look and feel.

He designs an innovative translucent staircase and gets the patent for it.

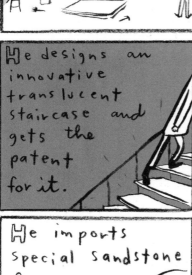

He imports special sandstone from Italy for the floors.

Ron Johnson

Steve, I have an idea. We can have experts on hand at a special counter and call them geniuses.

I don't like your idea. And they're geeks!

Chapter

**12**

Expansion

(2000 – 2004)

Steve, always trying to improve the Apple product consumer experience, develops a cable for digital data called firewire, and some cool new activities — called applications — like

iPhoto
iMovie
Final Cut Pro,
iDVD,
Garage Band
and...

iMAC

(What does the i-something stand for? Individual, instant, inform, inspire, and Internet)

# ... ¡iTunes!

Always a HUGE music fan (he loves the Beatles and Bob Dylan), Steve comes out with a clever new way to manage, mix, and enjoy music.

You can listen to your music on your computer and you can upload it, sort it, make playlists, and listen to the radio, too!

WOW — and visuals that go with the music! Cool! This comes included on the Mac when you buy it?

Too bad the portable music devices are all badly designed and user-unfriendly.

Back home and pining for Japanese food, Steve sends the Apple cafeteria chef to the Tsukiji Soba Academy in Japan for training.

TSUKIJI

With the new technology bought from Toshiba,

the tiny drives

Apple's designers and engineers work together on a SECRET new product.

What can it be?

A portable music player!
The others out there are #%&*@!!!
mini-disc player
(terrible interface!)
Rio
(ugly!)
Sony CD player
(too big and clunky!)
needs CDs

175

Yes, Steve can be ultra-convincing. If you've been told (unrealistically) that you can get the prototype out overnight or present 10 new ideas for the meeting tomorrow...

...you've entered Steve's famous "reality distortion field."

An engineer presents the prototype that he's been working on for weeks— day and night, night and day.

It's too heavy!

Too clunky!

See the bubbles coming up? There's AIR in there!

First Steve sells one record company on the idea. Then another comes on board.

Some ask for a % of iPod sales.

No way!

Some recording artists object:

No unbundling of MY albums!

My contract forbids that sort of thing.

NO deconstructing!

But it is too late. Everyone knows that piracy has been going on for months and Steve's innovations are necessary.

Steve travels around and shows off how easy it is to use the iTunes store.

iTunes

And then some musicians decide they really like the idea.

Looky, looky....Man, somebody FINALLY got it right!

iTunes

Recording artists and music producers finally sign on. Steve gets the record companies to sell their songs online in the iTunes store, and gets music lovers to pay for what they had been getting for free.

* Apple gets 29¢

This revolutionizes the music industry.

Chapter

13

COMPUTER

Refined

**DESIGN**

(2004-2011)

the family

Steve and Laurene now have 3 Kids.

REED 15

ERIN 11

EVE 8

Steve's impeccable design sense is not left at the office. At home, when it comes time to buy a new washer, meetings are held and pros and cons debated.

top loaders

front loaders

German

gentle on clothes

uses less water

soft clothes

American

most quiet **a** **b**

↳ uses least electricity **c**

needs more soap **d**

OK, so here's the final rundown....

I like QUIET!

Dad, does it come in turquoise?

192

193

196

Multi-touch* technology is being developed at Apple for a future tablet.

But when Steve sees his first demo of multi-touch on a phone, he decides to forge ahead and not hold the technology back.

*using more than one finger at a time to do fancy stuff, like enlarge an image

This is the future!!

This is it!!

Jony Ive

197

The CEO of Corning Glass makes a presentation.

Every year Steve unveils Apple's new products at Macworld, a trade show for Apple products.
mac WORLD 2007
Today we have 3 amazing products!
We have a wide-screen iPod with touch controls!
We have a revolutionary mobile phone!
And we have a breakthrough Internet communications device.
Are you getting it? It's just ONE device! Introducing the...
wow!
yes!
Because it is now a company that makes other products, Apple drops "computer" from its name.

Mobile phones spread worldwide.

What'

CANADA EURO AFRICA S.A. South Amer uth

Wi-Fi - connecting to Internet without cable

2 0

Google becomes a verb.

USBs

ebooks

Kindle N o o k

Once upon a time...

tablet - a handheld computer operated by a stylus or finger

New?

YouTube
Wikipedia
flash
technology

iMac
Sunflower

'00s

Global
Positioning
System

Amazon—
online retailing
blogs

Texting
catches
on.

Facebook
MySpace

iCloud,
a new way to
manage and sync
up data and
devices

Steve tries to keep his cancer battle a secret. He feels it's a personal matter, AND he's worried about the public losing confidence in Apple.

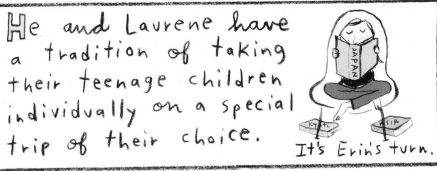

He and Laurene have a tradition of taking their teenage children individually on a special trip of their choice.

It's Erin's turn.

Steve is barely able to make it.

They travel to Japan and to a temple of 100 mosses.

Back home, Laurene tends a bountiful garden.

Steve works.

Steve's illness kills his appetite.

Your time is limited, so don't waste it living someone else's life.

Don't be trapped by dogma, which is living with the results of other people's thinking.

Don't let the noise of others' opinions drown out your own inner voice.

STANFORD UNIVERSITY

215

# Acknowledgments

Thanks to Anne, Lee, Rachael, and Stephanie at Schwartz & Wade Books; my agent, Brenda Bowen; David Biedny for a top-notch tech overview and history; Nick Sung for a terrific tour; my assistants, Ellspeth Tremblay and Dingding Hu; Isabelle Dervaux; Anne Silverstein; siblings Andrea and Sammy Recalde; the Bellport, New York, library; and my two favorite people in the world, Carl and Sam Friedberg.

# Bibliography

The teetering stack of material I've accumulated to write and illustrate this book is over four feet tall! In the pile are books, DVDs, photographs, maps, clippings, sketches, printouts, and magazines, including old copies of *Popular Electronics, Popular Mechanics,* and *Mechanix Illustrated* from the 1960s and 1970s. More specifically:

Brown, David W. "In Praise of Bad Steve." *The Atlantic,* October 6, 2011, theatlantic.com/technology /archive/2011/10/in-praise-of-bad-steve/246242/.

Elliot, Jay. *The Steve Jobs Way: iLeadership for a New Generation.* Philadelphia: Vanguard Press, 2011.

Goldsmith, Mike, and Tom Jackson. *Eyewitness COMPUTER.* New York: DK Publishing, 2011.

Goodell, Jeff. "Steve Jobs in 1994: The Rolling Stone Interview." *Rolling Stone,* June 16, 1994, rollingstone.com/culture/news/steve-jobs-in-1994-the-rolling-stone-interview-20110117.

Isaacson, Walter. *Steve Jobs.* New York: Simon and Schuster, 2011.

Jobs, Steve. Macworld Expo keynote address, 2007, youtube.com/watch?v=-QZKy9FzR6k.

———. Stanford University commencement address, June 12, 2005, youtube.com /watch?v=VHWUCX6osgM.

Manjoo, Farhad. "Jobs the Jerk." *Slate,* October 25, 2011, slate.com/articles/technology /technology/2011/10/steve_jobs_biography_the_new_book_doesn_t_explain_what_made _the_.html.

Markoff, John. "Apple Computer Co-Founder Strikes Gold with New Stock." *New York Times,* 30 November 1995, nytimes.com/1995/11/30/us/apple-computer-co-founder-strikes-gold -with-new-stock.html.

———. *What the Dormouse Said: How the Sixties Counterculture Shaped the Personal Computer Industry.* New York: Viking, 2005.

Moritz, Michael. *Return to the Little Kingdom: How Apple and Steve Jobs Changed the World.* New York: Overlook Press, 2009. Kindle edition.

Morris, Betsy. "Steve Jobs Speaks Out." *Fortune,* March 2008, money.cnn.com/galleries/2008 /fortune/0803/gallery.jobsqna.fortune/.

Morrow, Daniel. Smithsonian Institution Oral History interview with Steve Jobs, April 20, 1995, americanhistory.si.edu/comphist/sj1.html.

———. "Steve Jobs interview: One-on-one in 1995." *Computerworld,* April 1995, computerworld .com/s/article/9220609/Steve_Jobs_interview_One_on_one_in_1995.

Richards, Mark, and John Alderman. *Core Memory: A Visual Survey of Vintage Computers.* San Francisco: Chronicle Books, 2007.

Rosenbaum, Ron. "Secrets of the Little Blue Box," *Esquire,* October 1971, historyofphonephreaking .org/docs/rosenbaum1971.pdf.

Sheff, David. "Steven Jobs." *Playboy,* February 1985, longform.org/stories/playboy-interview-steve
-jobs.

*Triumph of the Nerds: The Rise of Accidental Empires.* Ambrose Video, 2002.

Wolf, Gary. "Steve Jobs: The Next Insanely Great Thing." *Wired,* February 1996, archive.wired.com
/wired/archive//4.02/jobs.html?person=steve_jobs&topic_set=wiredpeople.

To further research this book, and especially for the pictures, I visited Silicon Valley and drove on the 101 Freeway and along El Camino Real. I visited the Computer History Museum in Mountain View, and went to Palo Alto and the Stanford Linear Accelerator Laboratory. I saw where Xerox PARC once was, and I got a glimpse of the suburban garage in Los Altos where Apple Computer was born, as well as the Jobs family house in Palo Alto. Back up north in the San Francisco Bay Area, I was given a tour of Pixar. (Thanks, NS!)

# Notes

Any quotes not mentioned below in the source notes are made up, with an intent to communicate a sense of what I imagine was said.

"Here's to the crazy ones": advertising copy partly written by Steve Jobs.

## Chapter 1
On growing up in the early days of Silicon Valley: Isaacson, 1–20, and Smithsonian interview.
On middle-school teacher Imogen Hill: *Playboy* and *Computerworld*.
On Larry Lang: *Computerworld* and Smithsonian interview.

## Chapter 2
On building a frequency counter: *Playboy* and Isaacson, 17.

## Chapter 3
On the blue box: *Esquire*.
On building the blue box: Moritz, Chapter 6: "The Little Blue Box," and *Triumph of the Nerds*, Part 1.
On selling the blue boxes: *Playboy* and Isaacson, 29–30.

## Chapter 4
On being at Reed College: Isaacson, 33–41.
"If today were the last day": Stanford University commencement address.
"I'm going to find my": Isaacson, 45.
"Live each day as if": *Fortune*.
On meeting with Zen master Kobun: Isaacson, 48–50.

## Chapter 5
"Don't take no" and "Pretend to be": Isaacson, 55.
On computer history: the Computer History Museum, Goldsmith, and Richards.
On choosing a company name: Isaacson, 63, and Moritz, Chapter 10: "Half Right."
"I don't think it would have happened without": *Playboy*.

## Chapter 6
On Markkula: Isaacson, 75–78, and Moritz, Chapter 12, "Mercedes and a Corvette."
On the early days of Apple and first uses of Apple IIs: Moritz, Chapter 18, "Welcome IBM, Seriously."
"You should never start a company": Isaacson, 78.

## Chapter 7
On Xerox PARC: *Triumph of the Nerds*, Part 3.

## Chapter 8
"If it could save a person's": *Triumph of the Nerds*, Part 3.
"Do you want to spend the rest of": *Triumph of the Nerds*, Part 3.
"Good artists imitate": *Triumph of the Nerds*, Part 3. (Steve Jobs attributed this quote to Pablo Picasso.)
On being ousted from Apple: Isaacson, 194–210.
On NeXT: "It's not late": Isaacson, 236.

Chapter 9

On finding his biological family and on meeting Laurene Powell: Isaacson, 250–283.

Chapter 10

On the early days of Pixar: Isaacson, 238–249.

"There's no yacht": *New York Times*.

Chapter 11

"Which one do I tell": Isaacson, 337.

"What kind of computer would the Jetsons": Isaacson, 352.

"Did Alexander Graham Bell": Isaacson, 170.

"Henry Ford liked to say": Elliott, 147.

On the design of the first Apple Store: Isaacson, 368–377.

Chapter 12

"There's no satisfying clicking": *Slate*.

On the development of the iPod: Isaacson, 490–510.

On tossing an iPod prototype into a fish tank: *The Atlantic*.

"What's on your iPod?": Isaacson, 497.

Chapter 13

On the history of cell phones and development of the iPhone: Elliott, 203–204.

"The phone will have only one": Elliott, 23, and *Fortune*.

On the design of the iPhone: Isaacson, 465–475.

"This is the future!": Isaacson, 468.

"Every once in a while a revolutionary product comes along": Macworld Expo keynote address.

On appliance shopping: *Wired*.

On designing the family yacht: Isaacson, 529.

"Your time is limited": Stanford University commencement address.

# About the Author

Jessie Hartland is the author and illustrator of the highly acclaimed graphic biography *Bon Appétit: The Delicious Life of Julia Child,* which the *New York Times* described as "bursting with exuberant urban-naïf gouache paintings and a hand-lettered text that somehow manages to recount every second of Child's life." Her illustrations have appeared in newspapers and magazines throughout the world, including the *New York Times, Bon Appétit, Martha Stewart Living, Real Simple,* and *Travel + Leisure.* She is also a commercial artist whose work can be seen on ceramics and fabric, as well as in advertisements and store windows. She lives in New York City with her family. Visit her at jessiehartland.com.